The fron

What is th
this picture

Have you e
What did you have to do?

What does the title say?

The Perfect Pizza

Mum is ill, and Kate and Jack want to make a pizza with all her favourite toppings. But the pizza is a bit of a surprise to everyone!

The back cover

Let's read the blurb.

What toppings do you think Kate and Jack will choose?

Jane Langford
Illustrated by Shelagh McNicholas

The title page

Let's read the title again together.

Here is a little girl. Who might she be? What is she holding? What do you think these things are for?

The author of this book is Jane Langford and the illustrator is Shelagh McNicholas.

LESSON 1

READ

Read pages 2 and 3

Purpose: To find out what was wrong with Mum and what Kate and Jack decided to do about it.

EXPLORE

Pause at page 3

What was the matter with Mum? What did Kate and Jack decide to do?

How would making a pizza help Mum feel better?

Mum was ill.
She was in bed.

Jack and his little sister Kate
wanted to make Mum feel better.
"Let's make Mum a pizza," said Jack.

READ

Read pages 4 and 5

Purpose: To find out how to make a pizza.

EXPLORE

Pause at page 5

Who knows how to make a pizza? What does Jack say you have to do? What sort of toppings does Jack suggest? How will they find out what sort of pizza to make Mum?

Who can read the sentence that tells us they are going to ask Mum about her favourite pizza.

Look at the words 'pepperoni' and 'mushrooms'. Let's count how many syllables are in these words. (*Clap out the syllables with children as they say the words.*)

Tricky word (page 5):
The word 'pepperoni' may be beyond the children's word recognition skills. Tell this word to the children.

"How do you make pizza?" asked Kate.
"It's easy," said Jack.
"You make a pizza base,
then you add toppings."

4

"What are toppings?" asked Kate.
"They are your favourite things to eat,"
said Jack, "like pepperoni or mushrooms.
You can ask Mum what toppings she likes."

5

Read pages 6 and 7

Purpose: To find out what happened when Kate went
to ask Mum about her favourite sort of pizza.

Pause at page 7

What was Mum doing when Kate went upstairs?
What did Kate decide to do? What did Kate ask Dad?

Do you think chocolates are a good pizza topping?
What should Kate have asked Dad?

Identify the word 'chocolates'. Who can count the
number of syllables in this word?

Turn to page 15 for Revisit and Respond activities.

Kate went upstairs to ask Mum,
but Mum was fast asleep.
"I'll ask Dad," thought Kate.

Kate went to see Dad.
Dad was in the study.
"Dad, what is Mum's favourite thing
to eat?" asked Kate.
"Chocolates," said Dad.
"I saw some in a box up there."
Dad gave the box of chocolates to Kate.

LESSON 2

RECAP

Recap lesson 1

What has happened so far in the story?

What are the children trying to do?

READ

Read pages 8 and 9

Purpose: To find out who Kate saw next and what other food she got for her mum's pizza.

EXPLORE

Pause at page 9

What did Kate ask Grandma? What did Grandma say that Mum liked?

What did Mrs Price think Kate was doing?

What do you think Kate will do with the marshmallows and biscuits?

Find the question Kate asks Grandma. How do you know it is a question? Can you point out the question mark?

Tricky word (page 8):
The word 'marshmallows' may be beyond the children's word recognition skills. Tell this word to the children.

Tricky word (page 9):
The word 'biscuits' may also want to be discussed as a tricky word.

Kate went to see Grandma.
Grandma was in the garden.
"Grandma, what is Mum's favourite thing
to eat?" asked Kate.
"Marshmallows!" said Grandma.
"I have some in my pocket."
Grandma gave the marshmallows to Kate.

Then Mrs Price from next door
peeped over the fence.
"Are you having a picnic, Kate?"
asked Mrs Price.
"No," said Kate. "These are for Mum.
She's ill. She's in bed."
"Oh dear!" said Mrs Price.
"Here are some ginger biscuits for her.
Your mum loves ginger biscuits."

Read pages 10 to 12

Purpose: To find out what Kate and Jack did with the food Kate had been given.

Pause at page 12

What did Kate do with the food?

What question did Jack ask? What did Jack think Kate had done?

Was it Mum who chose these toppings?

What did Jack put on the pizza? Look at how the list is written. What do you notice between the words? (*a comma*)

If we write a list in a sentence, we always use a comma to separate the words in the list.

Kate went back to the kitchen.
She gave the chocolates, marshmallows,
and ginger biscuits to Jack.

10

"Chocolates, marshmallows, and ginger biscuits?
Are these Mum's favourite toppings?"
asked Jack.
"Yes!" said Kate.

11

Jack put the toppings on the pizza.
Then he put the pizza in the oven.

12

READ

Read pages 13 and 14

Purpose: To find out who came into the kitchen.

EXPLORE

Pause at page 14

Who came into the kitchen? Why did they come?

Would you enjoy eating this pizza? Why? Why not?

Do you think Mum will like the pizza? What does she say?

Who can find the word which describes the smell?

Soon, there was a wonderful smell.
Dad came into the kitchen.
Grandma came into the kitchen.
Mrs Price came into the kitchen.

13

Last of all, Mum came into the kitchen.
"What is that wonderful smell?" she asked.
"It's pizza," said Jack. "Try some."

14

"Mmmmm, chocolates," said Mum.
"Mmmmm, marshmallows.
Mmmmm, ginger biscuits!
My favourites!
Who chose the toppings?"

15

"THEY did!" said Kate.

16

READ

Read to the end

Purpose: To find out if Mum liked the pizza.

EXPLORE

Pause at page 16

Did Mum enjoy the pizza? What did Mum want to know?

How do you think Kate and Jack felt at the end? How do you think Mum felt?

What do you notice about the word 'They' on page 16? How does this mean we should say it? Let's read it again with expression.

After Reading
Revisit and Respond

Lesson 1

- What has happened so far in the story? Do you think Mum will like the pizza? Why/why not? What would you add to the pizza?

- Write on a whiteboard: '"Dad, what is Mum's favourite thing to eat?" asked Kate.' Ask the children to think of different ways of phrasing the question, so it still means the same (e.g. *What's Mum's favourite food? What does Mum like eating?*).

- Prepare a list of food words, including some from the text, e.g. *pepperoni, chocolate, pizza, mushrooms.* Ask children to count the syllables in each word. Then ask each child in the group to say a food word, clapping the syllables at the same time.

Lesson 2

- Ask the children to think about a time when they were ill. What did other people (Mum, Dad, sisters, brothers, etc), do to help them?

- Ask the children (using the list of food from last lesson) to help you write a sentence about going to the shops, e.g. 'We went to the shops and we bought eggs, chocolate, grapes, and butter.' Point out the commas in the list. Then ask them to write their own list, using individual whiteboards.

- Ask them to brainstorm and list words on another topic (e.g. *school – ruler, book, pencil case,* etc.) and repeat the syllable-clapping activity in groups (see lesson 1).

Follow-up

Independent Group Activity Work

This book is accompanied by two photocopy masters, one with a reading focus, and one with a writing focus, which support the teaching objectives of this book. The photocopy masters can be found in the Planning and Assessment Guide.

PCM F3.1 (*reading*)

PCM F3.2 (*writing*)

You may also like to invite the children to read the text again during their independent reading (either at school or at home).

Writing

Guided writing: Write a recipe, showing ingredients and method, of how to make a pizza. Use PCM F3.2.

Extended writing: Write an account of making your own favourite pizza.

Assessment Points

Assess that the children have learnt the main teaching points of the book by checking that they can:

- identify why certain things happen
- identify why characters change in the story (e.g. why Mum feels better).